FACTS ABOUT Cats & Dogs

By Jenny Phillips and Sue Stuever Battel

The Good AND THE Beautiful

Cover Design by Phillip Colhouer

Challenge Words

domestic

queen

balance

tongue

Egypt

A baby cat is called a kitten. Look closely at this kitten. Isn't she so cute?

Kittens cannot hear or see until they are one to three weeks old.

Kittens love to play,
chase things, and hunt.

This kitten thinks she can scare the flowers. The flowers are not scared.

This kitten thinks he is a great hunter. He will chase all the bugs he sees.

The kittens a mother has at one time is called a litter. Most litters have three to five kittens, but some can have more than ten kittens!

Kittens sleep a lot. It seems they can fall asleep in any place.

Just like people, cats
are either boys (males) or
girls (females).

Kittens purr as they drink milk from their mothers and as their mothers clean them.

Two-month-old kittens have 26 teeth. They lose their baby teeth when they are about six months old, and they get 30 grownup teeth.

Can a cat see better than you when it is dark? Yes! They see six times better than people in the dark. They can also hear and smell really well.

A cat hisses and arches its back when it is scared of something.

Walking without a sound, cats are good hunters. Sneaky and fast, they like to catch mice, birds, and crickets.

The tail of a cat tells how it feels. This cat feels happy.

This cat is scared.

This cat feels mad.

Cats can have long hair or short hair or no hair at all!

Domestic cats are the kind that live with people. Tigers, bobcats, and others are wild cats.

Cats take a bath by licking.
A mother cat licks her kittens
to keep them clean.

A father cat is called a tomcat. A mother cat is called a queen.

Cats have tails to help them balance. A cat lands on its feet when it falls.

This cat likes to hide in a box. It makes her feel safe.

Sharp claws help cats catch their food. They have claws on all four paws. Each front paw has five toes and each back paw has four toes.

Cats can be many colors: pretty orange, fuzzy brown, fluffy gray, sleek black, and soft white too! They can have many patterns.

If a cat is sick, you can take it to the vet. The vet will help your pet get better.

Cats are often pets, but they can also do good work. Cats catch mice. This helps farms, houses, and other places stay clean and safe.

People have had domestic cats as pets for many years. Even 4,000 years ago, people in Egypt had pet cats. Do you have a pet cat in your home?

Most orange tabby cats are male. This is because only one parent has to have orange in the family for an orange male kitten to be born. For an orange female kitten, both the mother and father must carry orange traits.

Calico cats have orange, black, and white fur. Almost every calico cat is female. This is because they must have a set of traits that only females can have.

Have you ever felt a cat's tongue? Did it scratch? The tongue has many sharp bumps on it. This is so the cat can clean itself and also so it can get meat off a bone.

Play is how kittens learn about the world. What other animals like to play to learn?

A kind of cat is called a breed. There are more than 70 breeds of cats.

Ragdoll

Siamese

Bengal

British Shorthair

Which cat on these pages do you like best?

Persian

Russian Blue

Scottish Fold

Sphynx

When a puppy is born, its eyes are shut. When baby humans are born, they can see right away.

Puppies chew because they are teething.

Like other mammals, puppies drink milk from their mothers.

Puppies are born in litters with sisters and brothers. Dogs often have three to eight puppies in a litter.

A puppy with big paws will probably grow up to be a very big dog. Will this puppy be big or small?

Puppies become adult dogs between nine and twenty-four months old. When you were nine to twenty-four months old, you were just a toddler!

It takes a lot of work to train a puppy. A puppy needs to learn where to go potty, what is OK to chew, and to not jump too much.

Puppies are born with no teeth. Then about 28 teeth grow in. At first, puppies eat soft food. Adult dogs have 42 teeth.

Older dogs chew to clean their teeth. It also helps them have strong jaws.

Dogs can be big or small.

Some dogs are good at hunting. Other dogs herd sheep and cows. Some are great pets.

Dogs can be good helpers to people. Leader dogs help blind people move around safely. Search and rescue dogs help find lost people.

Have you seen a dog smell the ground? A dog can smell up to one hundred thousand times better than a person.

Why do dogs sniff everything? Dogs get to know things through their noses. They say hello and learn about each other by smelling.

Domestic dogs are raised by people. Wild dogs live in the wild. The gray wolf and the red fox are kinds of wild dogs.

Dogs need a lot of time to run and play. This keeps them feeling good.

Always ask the owner before you pet a dog. Let it sniff your hand first. Then pet it on the back or sides.

Do not go up to a dog that looks scared or mad. It might not know if you are safe. It could bite.

Dogs can hear very well.
They can hear high sounds
that humans cannot hear.
They can also hear faraway
sounds.

Like cats, dogs eat meat in the wild. In your home they can eat dog food. Dog food is made from meat and other things.

Dogs can be good friends to people. Do you think this dog looks friendly?

Dogs need good care.
They need baths, trips to
the vet, and clipped nails.

Dogs can have many colors and patterns.

 Some have spots.

Some have

one color.

Some have

two or more colors.

They can have

marbled fur.

 They can

have brindle fur.

Many dogs have two layers of fur. The top layer is stiff hair. The underlayer is soft and warm.

Have you seen a dog pant with its tongue out? It does this to cool down. The dog puts its tongue out and breathes fast.

A dog can be trained to obey words. Dogs can learn words like sit, stay, come, and leave it.

Chocolate is not good for dogs. If a dog eats a little chocolate, it can throw up. If it eats a lot, it could get very sick or even die.

Dogs are nice pets. They are fun to play with and can be very loving!

Different breeds of dogs are known for different things.

Labrador Retriever

Shetland Sheepdog

German Shepherd

Siberian Husky

There are more than 400 dog breeds in the world. Which do you like best?

Poodle

Beagle

Miniature Schnauzer

Cocker Spaniel